AF228332

COUNTRIES ON THE WORLD STAGE

SPOTLIGHT ON

China

Isaac Kerry

Lerner Publications ◆ Minneapolis

Content consultant: Dr. Zhao Ma

Lerner Publications Company
An imprint of Lerner Publishing Group, Inc.
241 First Avenue North
Minneapolis, MN 55401 USA

For reading levels and more information, look up this title at www.lernerbooks.com.

Main body text set in Aptifer Sans LT Pro Semibold.
Typeface provided by Linotype AG.

Illustration on page 11 by Laura K. Westlund.
Flag on page 29 by Laura K. Westlund.

Designer: Athena Currier **Photo Editor:** Annie Zheng
Lerner team: Martha Kranes

Library of Congress Cataloging-in-Publication Data

Names: Kerry, Isaac, author.
Title: Spotlight on China / Isaac Kerry.
Description: Minneapolis, MN : Lerner Publications , [2023] | Series: Countries on the world stage | Includes bibliographical references. | Audience: Ages 8–12 | Audience: Grades 4–6 | Summary: "China is one of the world's oldest and most powerful countries. Discover China's history and how it became a global power. Then learn about its recent events, and look to the future of the country"— Provided by publisher.
Identifiers: LCCN 2022033212 (print) | LCCN 2022033213 (ebook) | ISBN 9781728491967 (library binding) | ISBN 9781728496467 (ebook)
Subjects: LCSH: China—Juvenile literature. | China—History—Juvenile literature.
Classification: LCC DS706 .K47 2023 (print) | LCC DS706 (ebook) | DDC 951—dc23/ eng/20220715

LC record available at https://lccn.loc.gov/2022033212
LC ebook record available at https://lccn.loc.gov/2022033213

Manufactured in the United States of America
1-53135-51145-11/10/2022

TABLE OF CONTENTS

A New Nation

MAO ZEDONG STEPS UP TO A MICROPHONE ON OCTOBER 1, 1949.

He stands on steps in Tiananmen Square staring out over a huge crowd. Mao is the leader of the rebel Chinese Communist Party. After a hard-fought civil war, his forces have won. He is ready to announce the founding of a new nation. The red flag of the People's Republic of China unfolds over the square. The soldiers of the People's Liberation Army march by to a new national anthem. China—and the world—will never be the same.

Mao declares the start of a new nation, the People's Republic of China, in 1949.

CHAPTER 1

China through the Ages

China is one of the oldest civilizations in the world. The Shang dynasty ruled China for over five hundred years from 1600–1046 BCE. It's China's earliest-known dynasty. Historians in China think there was an earlier dynasty but haven't found written records of it.

After the Shang dynasty fell, other dynasties would rise and rule China before they also fell. Some dynasties lasted hundreds of years. Sometimes many powerful kingdoms ruled China instead of just one kingdom. The Three Kingdoms era had three powerful states that ruled different

parts of the country. Ruling from 1644 to 1912, Qing was China's last dynasty. The Qing fought with several European countries and the rising Japanese Empire.

OPIUM WARS

Starting in the late 1700s, British merchants began bringing huge amounts of the drug opium into China. This caused addiction and suffering among the Chinese people. When the Qing government tried to stop this, Britain sent soldiers. They defeated the Qing army. Britain made several demands on China including taking the island of Hong Kong for the British Empire. This fighting was called the Opium Wars (1839–1842, 1856–1860).

A battle during the First Opium War

The Qing dynasty's fall led to the rise of the Republic of China. It had many different leaders over its short rule. The Chinese Communist Party (CCP) formed in 1921. The success of the Communist revolution in Russia inspired them. Soon they were a powerful force within China. They fought the government for power. Mao Zedong led the CCP. He led his forces against the Kuomintang, the main party that led the government. The CCP and Kuomintang forces fought many battles between 1927 and 1937 during the Chinese Civil War (1927–1949).

The CCP and the government declared a truce when Japan invaded in 1937. Once they defeated Japan in 1945, the fighting started again. Mao and the CCP declared victory in 1949. The new country would be the People's Republic of China. The CCP has controlled China's mainland ever since.

The CCP piles sandbags during the Chinese Civil War.

CHAPTER 2

A Tour of the Middle Kingdom

China is in East Asia. Spanning more than 3.7 million square miles (9.6 million sq. km), China is the third-largest nation. It borders fourteen countries including India, North Korea, Pakistan, Russia, and Vietnam.

China has almost every kind of terrain. It features mountain ranges, lush forests, huge grasslands, and several deserts. It has a long coast along the Pacific Ocean and includes many islands near its shores.

RUSSIA
KAZAKHSTAN
KYRGYZSTAN
MONGOLIA
NORTH KOREA
TAJIKISTAN
AFGHANISTAN
Great Wall of China
Beijing
北
CHINA
Shanghai
East China Sea
TIBET (Occupied by the PRC since 1950)
PAKISTAN
NEPAL
INDIA
BHUTAN
Hong Kong
Taiwan
INDIA
MYANMAR
LAOS
South China Sea
PACIFIC OCEAN
Miles
0 200 400 600
0 400 800
Kilometers
VIETNAM
INDIAN OCEAN
ARCTIC OCEAN
NORTH AMERICA
EUROPE
ASIA
ATLANTIC OCEAN
CHINA
AFRICA
PACIFIC OCEAN
SOUTH AMERICA
PACIFIC OCEAN
INDIAN OCEAN
AUSTRALIA
SOUTHERN OCEAN
Country capital
City
International border
Mountains
北 North (compass)

Mountains surround the
Five Flower Lake in Tibet.

EXPLORE THE GREAT WALL(S) OF CHINA

One of China's most famous features is the Great Wall of China (*below*). The Great Wall is actually several different walls. They were constructed over the course of two thousand years, mostly in northern China, stretching for over 5,500 miles (8,851 km)! These walls were made to protect the country from attacks.

China is the most populous nation in the world. Over 1.4 billion people live in China. That is over 18 percent of the world's population!

Shanghai is the largest city in China.

About 65 percent of the people in China live in cities. China has some of the largest cities in the world. Shanghai is the world's third most populated city with more than 26 million people. China's capital, Beijing, has a population of over 21 million. It's the ninth-largest city in the world.

China's population includes over fifty-six ethnic groups. Over 91 percent of the country's citizens belong to the Han ethnic group. The Han is the largest ethnic group on Earth. Some ethnic groups face discrimination. The Uyghurs are an ethnic group that follow Islam. Twelve million Uyghurs live in China. More than one million of them have been forced into incarceration camps. They are held against their will because of their identity. Journalists discovered these camps in 2017.

A Uyghur family celebrates Eid al-Fitr with food and traditional clothing.

CHAPTER 3

A Changing Economy

When the **CCP** took power in 1949, they had big plans for the country's economy. Its economy relied on farming. Mao wanted to focus on building and operating factories and businesses. This policy, called the Great Leap Forward, had some major effects. A large number of people were recruited to work in factories and there weren't enough people to harvest the country's crops. This led to a famine. An estimated thirty million people, primarily from the poorer rural regions, died.

Workers assemble cars in a Chinese factory.

EXPLORING MAOISM

Maoism is the political philosophy developed by Mao Zedong. Early on, the CCP took lessons from communism in the Soviet Union, a former country that included Russia. But Mao didn't like all the layers of government in the Soviet Union. He focused on engaging citizens to join his cause.

After Mao's death in 1976, a new group of leaders took over led by Deng Xiaoping. They wanted to reform the country's economy. They believed that the Communist economy had limited the nation's economic growth. One part of communism they wanted to change was how much control the government had over the economy. Over the next several years, the government encouraged the growth of private

Deng Xiaoping (*right*) led China from 1979 to 1992.

companies and allowed foreign investment. This made China an important part of the global supply chain.

These reforms continued over the years. In the 1980s, they had a major impact on the country's economy. Since then, the economy has grown by almost 10 percent every year. Over eight hundred million people are no longer in poverty. Two of the biggest parts of China's economy are manufacturing and agriculture. Many companies all over the world have their products made in China. The finished goods are then shipped overseas.

One-Party Rule

Since 1949 the CCP has controlled China's government. More than ninety million people are members. Membership has many benefits, including consideration for important jobs in the party.

Every five years a National Party Congress elects a Central Committee. From the Central Committee a smaller Politburo is selected. These powerful individuals determine the policies that shape the country. The CCP has a tight control

One of China's political groups, the Chinese People's Political Consultative Conference, meets in 2019.

over media and information in the country. It does not allow its citizens to say negative things in public and on social media about the government.

TIANANMEN SQUARE MASSACRE

In May 1989 more than a million Chinese citizens joined a protest (*below*) in Beijing. The protesters, mostly students, wanted more individual rights. They peacefully protested for almost five weeks. In early June the Chinese army and police attacked the gathering. The Chinese government said that two hundred people died. Some journalists think the number could be much higher. At least ten thousand were arrested. The Chinese government still blocks all discussion of the event.

Deng Xiaoping led China after Mao's death. He is responsible for many of the economic reforms that helped China grow. He also created a rule where presidents could only serve two five-year terms. This was to make sure one person did not gather too much power as Mao had.

Xi Jinping (*center*) attends a meeting in 2017.

Xi Jinping was elected president in 2013. He made it harder for people in government to take money from China's citizens. But he also made himself more powerful. In 2018 Xi convinced the National People's Congress to get rid of term limits for the presidency. So, Xi or someone else can be elected president as long as they win elections. Xi was reelected president in 2018 for five more years.

China in the Twenty-First Century

MODERN CHINA IS A POWERFUL COUNTRY. Its influence extends far past its borders. China's economic growth means it could become a larger economy than the United States by 2030. But economic development comes with costs, such as severe pollution. As with the rest of the world, China struggled with the COVID-19 pandemic. They have tried to stop the spread of COVID, but that often means locking down cities. Then people can't go to work, which impacts the country's economy.

China has several different conflicts with neighboring countries. It claims that Taiwan is part of China. Taiwan has been a self-ruled island since the Kuomintang retreated there in 1949 and wants to stay separate. China has threatened the island with military force.

The president of Taiwan, Tsai Ing-wen, speaks in 2022.

CHINA EXPLORES MARS

China is committed to becoming a leader in space exploration. On May 14, 2021, the Zhurong rover (*below*) landed on Mars. The rover uses a special radar to search for signs of water. China is only the second country in the world to land a rover on Mars. In 2033 China plans to send astronauts to the Red Planet.

The British Empire controlled Hong Kong after the Opium Wars. In 1997 Hong Kong returned to China's rule. But the people of Hong Kong did not have a choice. China decided that people in mainland China and Hong Kong would have

People in Hong Kong protest on January 1, 2020, for more political freedom.

different rules. In Hong Kong, people have more freedoms. In 2019 a proposed bill could have limited the rights of Hong Kong's citizens. People protested. Many people in Hong Kong want to govern themselves, while China wants to control the city.

China's economy continues to grow. The world has been amazed by its growth and is waiting to see what China does next.

TIMELINE

1600–1046 BCE The first-recorded dynasty, the Shang, rules China. They are known for their use of calendars, advancements in astronomy and math, and casting bronze objects.

1644 The Qing dynasty begins its rule of China. They will be the last dynasty to control the country.

1839–1842 The Qing dynasty attempts to stop the flow of opium into their country. The British Empire responds with soldiers, and the First Opium War begins. The Qing lose and are forced to give Hong Kong to Britain.

1912 The Qing dynasty ends, and the Republic of China begins. A rapid succession of rulers and internal conflict occur.

1921 The Communist Party of China is founded. They initially work with the Kuomintang, but eventually the two enter into armed conflict.

1937 Japan invades China, starting the Second Sino-Japanese War. The CCP and Kuomintang work to fight off Japan.

1949 On October 1, Mao announces victory in the Chinese Civil War, and the People's Republic of China is founded. Nationalist leaders retreat from Taiwan.

1989 Hundreds of thousands of soldiers attack pro-democracy protesters in Tiananmen Square on June 4. Hundreds are killed and thousands arrested.

1997 Hong Kong is returned to China on July after over 150 years of British rule.

2008 China hosts the Beijing Summer Olympics.

2021 China sends a rover to Mars.

CHINA FAST FACTS

Name: People's Republic of China

Population: 1,450,175,077

Land area: 3,747,877 square miles (9,706,957 sq. km)

Largest city: Shanghai, population 28,516,904

Capital city: Beijing, population 21,333,332

Form of government: Communist Party-led state

Official language: Mandarin Chinese

Flag:

GLOSSARY

agriculture: farming

citizen: someone that lives in a country

communism: a system in which a government owns what is used to make and transport goods. In a Communist country, there is no privately owned property.

dynasty: a family of rulers who rule over a country for a long time

economy: the wealth and resources of a country, particularly the goods and services that are made, sold, and bought

ethnic: a group who has the same customs, religion, origin, and other similarities

famine: when many people do not have enough food to eat

government: the people who control and make decisions for the country

incarceration: being in prison

pollution: making land, water, or air dirty

rover: a vehicle used for exploring the surface of a moon or planet

LEARN MORE

Bjorklund, Ruth, and Sloane Gould. *China*. New York: Cavendish Square, 2023.

Ducksters: Ancient China for Kids
https://www.ducksters.com/history/china/ancient_china.php

Ducksters: Mao Zedong Biography
https://www.ducksters.com/biography/world_leaders/mao_zedong.php

Goldsworthy, Steve. *China*. New York: Lightbox Learning, 2021.

Kiddle: China Facts for Kids
https://kids.kiddle.co/China

Kids World Travel Guide: China Facts
https://www.kids-world-travel-guide.com/china-facts.html

Layton, Christine. *Travel to China*. Minneapolis: Lerner Publications, 2022.

Reynolds, Donna. *Ancient China Revealed*. New York: Cavendish Square, 2023.

INDEX

PHOTO ACKNOWLEDGMENTS

Image credits: AP Photo, p. 5; Wikimedia Commons PD, p. 7; Historical Images Archive/Alamy Stock Photo, p. 8; Keystone/Stringer/Hulton Archive/Getty Images, p. 9; Efired/Shutterstock, p. 12; zhu difeng/Shutterstock, p. 13; LMspencer/Shutterstock, p. 14; SolStock/E+/Getty Images, p. 15; Pradit.Ph/Shutterstock, p. 17; AP Photo/Neal Ulevich, p. 18; chinahbzyg/Shutterstock, p. 19; AP Photo/Zhejiang Daily – Imaginechina, p. 21; Peter Turnley/Archive Photos/Getty Images, p. 22; Drop of Light/Shutterstock, p. 23; SOPA Images/LightRocket/Getty Images, p. 25; China News Service/Getty Images, p. 26; Hsiuwen Liu/Shutterstock, p. 27.

Design elements: Bluemoon 1981/Shutterstock; StudioProX/Shutterstock; vectortatu/Shutterstock.

Cover: ZUMA Press/Alamy Stock Photo.